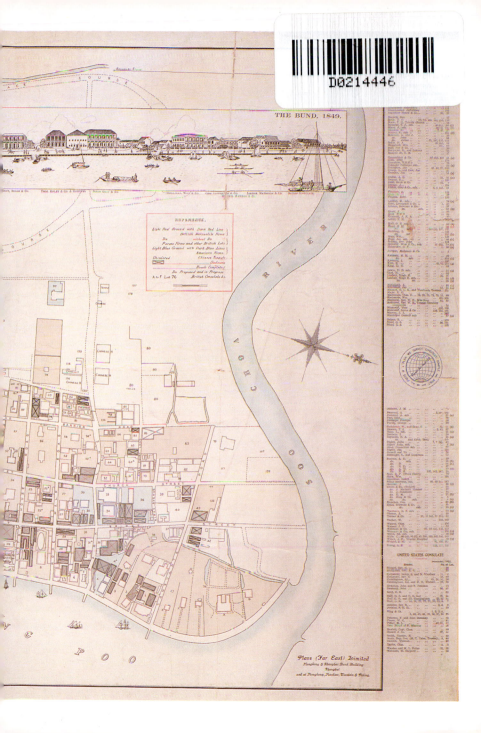

THE BUND, 1849.

Old Shanghai

TITLES IN THE SERIES

Series Editors, China Titles:

NIGEL CAMERON, SYLVIA FRASER-LU

Old Shanghai

Betty Peh-T'i Wei

OXFORD
UNIVERSITY PRESS

OXFORD
UNIVERSITY PRESS

Oxford University Press is a department of the University of Oxford.
It furthers the University's objective of excellence in research, scholarship,
and education by publishing worldwide in

Oxford New York

Athens Auckland Bangkok Bogotá Buenos Aires Calcutta
Cape Town Chennai Dar es Salaam Delhi Florence Hong Kong Istanbul
Karachi Kuala Lumpur Madrid Melbourne Mexico City Mumbai
Nairobi Paris São Paulo Singapore Taipei Tokyo Toronto Warsaw

with associated companies in Berlin Ibadan

Oxford is a registered trade mark of Oxford University Press

Published in the United States
by Oxford University Press Inc. New York

British Library Cataloguing in Publication Data
available

Library of Congress Cataloguing-in-Publication Data
Wei, Betty Peh-T'i, 1930–
Old Shanghai / Betty Peh-T'i Wei.
p. cm. — (Images of Asia)
Includes bibliographical references and index.
ISBN 0-19-585747-X
1. Shanghai (China) – History. I. Title. II. Series.
DS796.S257W44   1992
951'. 132–dc20
92–39412
CIP

Printed in Hong Kong
Published by Oxford University Press (China) Ltd
18th Floor Warwick House East, Taikoo Place, 979 King's Road,
Quarry Bay, Hong Kong

For Richard M. Liu,
who was born in Shanghai,
and our daughters
Katharine and Phebe

Preface

AT midnight on 28 January 1932, after a period of intensive negotiations with Chinese authorities in Shanghai and international organizations everywhere, Japanese planes dropped incendiary bombs on Chapei (Zhabei). The bombs destroyed railway tracks and devastated much of this industrial district in the north-west of Shanghai. Great losses were inflicted on both life and property. Residents of the foreign settlements, however, were more worried by the possible implications of the bombing, for the settlements had been havens from the violence and vagaries of international politics and domestic upheavals for some ninety years. Was this attack a signal that the good old days of Shanghai were coming to an end?

The answer is that, although the incident in January 1932 could have led to the immediate demise of an era, the actual end of the privileged days was not to arrive for another decade. A series of major events—the second Sino-Japanese War (1937–45), World War II, and the Communist victory resulting in the establishment of the People's Republic in October 1949—was to take place before the final disappearance of a lifestyle now known collectively as Old Shanghai. In the narrower sense, Old Shanghai, therefore, comprises the 106 years when foreigners enjoyed certain privileges in China.

Myths and legends about Old Shanghai are legion. That the port came into international renown as a result of the Opium War of 1840 and long thrived on commerce, including the opium trade and its corollary, vice and gambling, is a fact that cannot be denied. For more than a century, Shanghai was one of the leading port cities in the world where men grew rich by exploiting both opportunities and their fellow human beings. It was common knowledge that Shanghai was a smuggler's paradise where everything could be had for a price. Less well-known was information concerning government: that law-making and administration of the International Settlement were controlled by a few influential residents, with little or no interference from the British or Chinese governments. The French government did retain control in the French Concession through its consul at Shanghai. In neither settlement, however, was the Chinese population consulted on legislative or administrative matters until the 1920s.

The arrival of the British consul in November 1843 marked Shanghai's beginning as an international metropolis. Although already a city in the Chinese context and a busy port for domestic and foreign trade for several hundred years, at that time Shanghai could boast no more than 300,000 inhabitants. Ninety years later, in February 1934, it had a population of 3,350,570 Chinese and foreigners. By then, the port had developed into the commercial, financial, industrial, and cultural centre of modern China—its gateway to the outside world. In 1949, when the People's Republic was proclaimed, Shanghai was producing one-fifth of the country's industrial output, and two-thirds of its foreign trade was passing through the port.

André Malraux decried in *Man's Fate* the ills of a society which was growing economically prosperous but ignored great human misery. He was writing in reaction to the massacre of Communists and left-wing labour unionists in Shanghai in 1927. Chinese writers and social critics of that era, such as Lao She, through his novel *The Rickshaw Boy*, also brought to public attention the deep physical and mental suffering of the populace in Chinese cities. Contemporary film makers in Shanghai, too, could understand the underlying problems of their society; cinematic heroes were poor but virtuous, while villains were rich, cruel, and self-serving.

At the same time, there was a great deal of glamour and sophistication. Nocl Coward wrote *Private Lives* depicting an urbane society while he was ensconced in the Cathay Hotel overlooking The Bund and Shanghai harbour. Even Hollywood film makers picked up the theme of the mysterious but sinister image of Shanghai in *The Shanghai Express*, starring the svelte, young Marlene Dietrich and featuring the equally sensual and attractive Anna May Wong. These works were perhaps as unrepresentative of Shanghai society as Mark Twain's *Tom Sawyer* or F. Scott Fitzgerald's *The Great Gatsby* was typical of American people, but they did show that Shanghai was embedded in international consciousness as a wordly city of significance.

Contents

Acknowledgements

I am grateful to the following institutions and individuals for their generosity in giving permission to reproduce rare and often unique paintings and photographs from their collections: Alisan Fine Arts Ltd, Hong Kong and Alice King, Managing Director; Christie's Swire (Hong Kong) Ltd and Alice Piccus, Director; the Commercial Press (Hong Kong) Limited; the Hongkong and Shanghai Banking Corporation Group Archives and Margaret Lee, Manager; the Jardine Matheson Group and Elaine Ho, Archivist; the Swire Group and Maisie Shun Wah, Public Relations Manager; Cherry Barnett; Raymond and Isabel Chao; Fred and Ruby Chow; Samuel Chu; Lala Diestel; Suzy Moser, whose father John Moser found at a sidewalk sale in the south-west United States photographs taken by an unknown sailor on leave in Shanghai and Peking (Beijing) in 1919; and my sister-in-law Lee Wei.

My very special thanks go to Carl Smith, who graciously allowed me access to his unique collection of materials on the China coast communities; Samuel Chu, Ian Donaldson, Nigel Rich, and Professor Tang Zhenchang, who introduced to me sources of old photographs; and to Margaret Lee and her staff at the HKSBC Group Archives, who, in addition to tolerating my browsing through their collections, made suggestions concerning other resources. To the late Professor Sun Mingjing of the Institute of Cinematography in Beijing and Lloyd Chao of Golden Harvest Communications in Hong Kong, Frank and Shirley Chen, May Koon, David Lew, Mimi Young Ma, and Harry Rolnick, I also offer my thanks. The work of K. K. Sze of the University of Hong Kong Library in reproducing black and white photographs for publication is much appreciated.

I have included a chapter on Shanghai before the Opium War (1840–42) because I feel that the previous centuries had prepared the place and the people for the presence of foreigners in their midst, and for the acceptance of new institutions, standards, and values introduced from an alien civilization.

Chapter 5 is based on a paper I wrote for presentation at the International Symposium on Urban Studies held in Shanghai in November 1991 to mark the 700th anniversary of the founding of the city. It is included here as a memorial to the late Hans Diestel, who was born in Shanghai and was very much an active member of the community before 1949.

I have opted for the traditional romanized spellings for names of Chinese people and places, but a transliteration in the more contemporary *pinyin* system follows in parenthesis when a name is first introduced, as well as in the Index/Glossary.

Photo Credits

Alisan Fine Arts Ltd: Plate 7; Cherry Barnett: Plates 9, 13; Raymond and Isabel Chao: Figures 4.1, 4.10; Fred and Ruby Chow: Plate 1; Christie's Swire (Hong Kong) Limited: Plates 3, 4; Samuel Chu: Figure 4.8; The Commerical Press (Hong Kong) Limited: Figures 1.4, 6.1; Lala Kammerling Diestel: Figures 4.3, 4.4, 4.6; Hongkong and Shanghai Banking Corporation Group Archives: Endpapers, Plates 2, 6, 14; Figures 1.2, 2.1, 6.2, 6.3; Shanghai of Today: Cover, Figures 1.1, 3.1, 3.2, 3.5, 4.3, 4.5, 5.1; Betty Wei Liu: Plates 8, 10, 11, 12, 15, 16; Suzy Moser: Figure 4.7; The Swire Group: Plate 5, Figures 3.3, 3.4; Lee Kung Wei: Figure 4.9

1

Early Shanghai

RECENT archaeological findings have revealed that much of the area that is now metropolitan Shanghai was under water as recently as 6,000 years ago. On the higher ground, however, there was wildlife, including elephants and roebuck, a hornless deer. Finds from a 5,000-year old cemetery reveal the existence of an agricultural community where there was clearly a division of labour between men and women. Men farmed, fished, and hunted while women spun and kept livestock. This society appears to have been matrilineal as five generations of women who died at different times were buried in a single tomb, together with children who had not reached adulthood. Men, on the other hand, were interred alone, with objects of daily use, simple stone or iron tools, and cauldrons, jars, and basins made of pottery. Vessels of bronze were few, but jade was already placed in the mouths of the dead. Pork was a regular item on the family menu, as were chicken and deer. Rice was in evidence. Dogs were kept as domestic animals.

Professor Linda Cooke Johnson of Michigan State University in her studies on pre-modern Shanghai disclosed that 'the first solid historical evidence for [Shanghai's] existence comes from the Tang dynasty.' Traditional accounts, however, claim that civil authorities of the Chinese Empire had been present in the region much earlier. Sun Ch'üan (Sun Quan) (d. AD 251), one of the leading protagonists of the Three Kingdoms period, controlled the area during the third century AD. The Lunghua (Longhua) pagoda, still standing in Shanghai today, is reputed to have been built under his aegis (Fig. 1.1). In reality, however, the present pagoda was

1

1.1
Lunghua pagoda, said to have been built originally in the third century AD by Sun Ch'üan to honour his nurse

not constructed until some time during the tenth century, supporting Professor Johnson's thesis that the area did not come into existence as a thriving community until around that time. This dating also serves as an indication that, by this time, there was sufficient wealth and cultural awareness in the area for residents to indulge in religious and artistic patronage.

There was a tremendous surge in the population of the lower Yangtze (Yangzi) River in the tenth century as the area gained importance as an agricultural centre. Water control projects had drained the marshes of the lower Yangtze and added significantly to the total land areas devoted to paddy farming. It was during this time that what is now metropolitan Shanghai emerged as dry land. Canals that had been in existence for local communication were further dredged and lengthened to connect with other waterways. A new strain of rice was introduced, making it possible to plant two crops each growing season. Consequently, by the time the Sung (Song) dynasty had established itself at the end of the tenth century, the lower Yangtze was already a cultural and economic centre of the Chinese Empire.

Several reasons led to the rise of Shanghai as a centre of trade at this time. During the earlier part of the tenth century, the imperial court discontinued the policy of favouring agriculture and discriminating against trade. As a result, during the eleventh century, Shanghai grew in importance as the area's residents turned to handling and transporting goods. Traders began to congregate along the western bank of the Whangpoo (Huangpu) River, gaining sufficient strength to form a guild of their own during the twelfth century.

Meanwhile, the Whangpoo River was widening, creating a deep harbour where it met the Woosung (Wusong), thereby enabling Shanghai to become a port at a later date. Silting of the inland waterways, including the Grand Canal, made it necessary for ships engaging in coastal and maritime trade to dock on the banks of the Whangpoo to discharge and take on cargo. At the same time, the central government began to transport tribute grain by sea. Shanghai became important in this respect as rice barges had to pass through the Whangpoo to reach the sea. The Bund, later a major thoroughfare of the foreign community in Shanghai, was originally a towpath made by coolies pulling barges along the river at this time.

Furthermore, advancement in navigation and ship-building techniques had made it possible for Chinese traders to meet the increasing overseas demand for the silk and porcelain produced in the Yangtze valley. Shanghai, accessible to both the Yangtze and the sea, began to develop into an entrepôt for coastal and maritime shipping in addition to being a market town for inter-regional trade. Even so, Shanghai never attained the sophistication of other lower Yangtze cities such as Yangchow (Yangzhou) and Soochow (Suzhou), but, in 1267, an office of the Superintendency of Foreign Trade was established on the western bank of the Whangpoo.

In 1291, Shanghai was officially established as a county, an administrative city in the Chinese context. Five villages were consolidated by the central government of the new Yuan dynasty as it embarked on an extensive programme to reorganize the administration of the empire. One of these villages was called Shang-hai, literally meaning 'above the sea'. From this village, the Yuan county as well as the modern city, received its name.

Towards the end of the fourteenth century, it became clear that the dominant features of the area's economy would be textiles and trade. The south bank of the lower Yangtze had been a major silk production centre for several hundred years. The introduction of cotton from the provinces of Kwangtung (Guangdong) and Fukien (Fujian) had provided another marketable product. The proliferation of cotton led to the development of a cottage industry of cotton textiles as the populace sought to supplement their income by working at home. At the end of the Yuan dynasty a peasant woman known as Huang Tao-p'o, (Haung Daopo) is said to have brought to the Shanghai area the skills of spinning and weaving cotton she had learned from the Li people of Hainan Island off the coast of Kwangtung. The value of Huang's contributions was readily recognized as a stone stele, glorifying her achievements in construct-

4

ing the machinery necessary for cotton weaving as well as matching coloured yarns to form intricate designs, was erected in her honour when she died (Fig. 1.2).

1.2 A mid-nineteenth century woman at a loom, but cotton spinning and weaving was an important cottage industry in the Shanghai area from the thirteenth century.

This commercialization of cotton meant that more and more arable land was turned over to cotton growing, further exhausting the soil. As a result, fertilizer as well as foodstuffs had to be brought to the area. A late Ming dynasty gazetteer reveals that the county held food supplies for only ten days at a given time. Rice, oil, beans, and wine were imported by the end of the dynasty, mostly from the middle Yangtze provinces. Fertilizer, found by Professor

Johnson to be soybean refuse, on the other hand, was 'imported from Shandong and Guandong [Liaodong].' Meanwhile, the shipping of goods to and from the area led to the rise of the transportation industry.

The maturity of Shanghai as an urban centre during the sixteenth century is demonstrated by the construction of a city wall at that time. With the concentration of business activities, communities along the river had become decidedly urban. At the same time, inhabitants and merchants needed protection from coastal pirates. The wall, curved to conform to the bend of the Whangpoo River, was completed in 1554. Surrounded by a moat, with enough space on the ramparts to accommodate men and single-wheeled carts—a favoured mode of transport which persisted into the twentieth century—the wall was ten metres high and roughly five kilometres in circumference.

Streets and buildings sprang up wherever the need arose. The streets were narrow, lined on both sides by one or two-storey houses of mud or wood used by their occupants as living quarters as well as places to transact business. Trades of the same nature tended to congregate together, resulting in such street names as Jade Alley, Medicine Street, or Silversmiths' Lane; a number of which have survived into the modern era.

The most important buildings were older than the city wall, but the major extant temples were constructed or extensively renovated during the Ming era. As can be expected from such a community, the Queen of Heaven, T'ien-hou (Tianhou) who guarded those who sailed on the waters, commanded an imposing edifice to house her image. The Temple of the City God, Ch'eng-huang (Chenghuang), growing more impressive with time, was located near the centre of the city.

A short distance away a lakeside tea pavilion flourished. At a later date this was called the Willow Tea-house by foreign residents because of the willow-patterned porcelain used there. Protected from the hustle and bustle of urban confusion by a symbolic zigzag bridge, to protect the multi-storeyed tea-house from evil spirits, patrons could gather for a few moments of respite or to transact business away from the constant interruptions in their shops.

During the seventeenth and eighteenth centuries, the economy of the Shanghai area continued to be dominated by cotton and transportation. Ships which brought food-stuffs and fertilizers to Shanghai from the hinterland carried away cotton textiles made by the local cottage industry. Merchants travelled to the off-shore islands fringing the Chinese coast to exchange porcelain, silk, and cotton tex-tiles with Japanese traders for copper and other commodities.

The Chinese tradition of an officialdom composed of scholars demanded intellectual accomplishments. Shanghai, a commercial port without any notable intellectual her-itage, was unable to claim many native sons of scholarly achievement during the imperial era, although there were institutions of learning in the outskirts such as Chia-ting (Jiading), now a suburb of metropolitan Shanghai. The Confucian temple, built there in the thirteenth century to signify the presence of learning, still stands, and includes a fine replica of a traditional civil examination hall. Its gar-den also serves as a demonstration of the high standard of living in the Shanghai area during Ming and early Ch'ing (Qing) dynasty times.

One of the few men of Shanghai who did rise to both scholarly and political prominence was Hsu Kuang-ch'i (Xu Guangqi) (1562–1633) who in 1623, despite conversion to Roman Catholicism, became Grand Secretary in the Ming government. It was he who brought the first European Jesuit missionaries to Shanghai, followed by priests of various nationalities, including French. Based on their missionary activities of this era the French government of the nineteenth century claimed the right to possess land in Shanghai.

Hsu also played an important role in bringing Western knowledge to China. The first Chinese scholar to translate books from European languages, his personal contributions included Euclid's *Elements*. He was also responsible for modernizing the Chinese calendar, and persuading the court to buy cannon through Portuguese traders in Macau. As early as 1608 Hsu invited Jesuit missionaries to start a Roman Catholic congregation in Shanghai and to build a church within the city wall. His grand-daughter, Candida (1607–80), is reputed to have followed his example by sponsoring more than one hundred chapels in the Shanghai area. The St Ignatius Cathedral, seat of the Roman Catholic Bishop and built in 1906, still stands in the Siccawei (Xujiahui) district of Shanghai.

British traders had long sought to expand their activities beyond Canton (Guangzhou), to which all foreign trade (except Russian) was confined before the Opium War of 1840–42. In 1832, an East India Company ship, *Lord Amherst*, with Charles Gutzlaff (1803–51) as interpreter, arrived at Shanghai, hoping to negotiate with local officials to open the port to British trade, but they were not successful. Henry Medhurst (1796–1857), the British missionary who, among his many achievements, played a significant role in the founding of the foreign community in Shanghai immediately after the Opium War, pronounced it to be 'one of the greatest emporiums of commerce on the east coast of China.' Moreover, Medhurst visualized Shanghai as an important port in the future development of international trade because of its location. '[Shanghai] communicates immediately with the rich districts of Soochow and Hang-chow, receiving silk brocades from the Acadia of China and conveying hither the inventions and commodities of the western world.'

Towards the end of the 1830s, the Chinese court debated whether to relax trade restrictions, but instead decided to tighten control, especially over opium. They also took measures to strengthen coastal defences. British traders increased their smuggling activities as they convinced their government to amass naval and military support to advance their interests in China. When the Opium War finally took place, the British forces proved too strong for the Chinese resulting in British victories in the Pearl River Delta, as well as along the Yangtze. The Treaty of Nanking was signed in August 1842. Under its terms Hong Kong was ceded to Britain, and five coastal ports, including Shanghai, were opened to British trade. In Shanghai, land along the Whangpoo River was set aside for British use. The first British consul arrived in November 1843, followed speedily by traders of various nations and Christian missionaries of different denominations. From that time onwards, the development of Shanghai became an international undertaking.

It was the strategic location of the port that had attracted the trade-minded British diplomats to negotiate for an area outside the Chinese city of Shanghai. Situated at the confluence of the Whangpoo River and Soochow Creek, and connected to the Yangtze River and the Grand Canal, Shanghai commanded access by water to all parts of China as well as to the rest of the world. Its deep and protected harbour was an added advantage (Fig. 1.3). The Treaty of Nanking gave British nationals the 'convenience of abode' at Shanghai, while stipulating that the Chinese government would accept

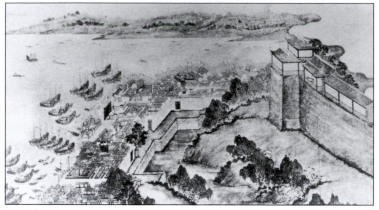

1.3 Shanghai harbour at the time of the Opium War. Ink painting by an unknown Chinese artist, *c.*1840.

1.4
The Right Reverend William J. Boone, the first bishop of the Episcopal Church in China and founder of the American settlement.

extra-territoriality and refrain from interfering with foreign trade. France, too, garnered similar concessions from the Chinese government in 1849; a prize which only encouraged other powers to extract comparable privileges from Chinese officials. The *laissez faire* policy of the British also allowed other nationals to live in the British settlement in Shanghai. For a while, there was an informal settlement for Americans, but this later merged with the British settlement to form the International Settlement (Fig. 1.4).

These areas of foreign residence eventually evolved into the International Settlement and the French Concession; both outside the walls of the old Chinese city of Shanghai and beyond the jurisdiction of the Chinese officials. In time, the three components: the Chinese city, the International Settlement, and the French Concession—as well as the surrounding countryside—became absorbed into what is now known as metropolitan Shanghai.

Further foreign incursions into China throughout the remainder of the nineteenth century enhanced the growth of Shanghai. As foreign troops continued to overpower Chinese imperial forces, the Chinese government opened more ports along the coast and the Yangtze River to foreign trade and residence. By the 1860s, Shanghai, with its favourable location and protected harbour, surpassed other treaty ports to become the leading centre of foreign commerce in China. In addition, as Chinese resources began to be developed on a large scale during the latter part of the century, business interests in Shanghai—isolated to a great extent from the political upheavals and military disturbances besetting the rest of China—were able to turn Shanghai into a financial and industrial centre as well.

2

People and Government

Initially, no ordinary Chinese who was not employed in a foreign household was allowed to live in the foreign settlements of Shanghai. Mid-nineteenth century rebellions against the Ch'ing dynasty, however, brought massive Chinese immigration into the settlements. In time, many young Chinese received a western-style education at schools and colleges established by foreign missionaries, such as Aurora University in the French Concession and St John's University in the International Settlement. A number went on to study abroad. These Western-educated Chinese played an increasingly important role, especially after 1912, in the development of Shanghai into a modern banking, commercial, industrial, and cultural centre, as well as a port of international stature.

The International Settlement, created in 1863, combined an enlarged British settlement and the informal American settlement in Hongkew (Hongkou) across Soochow Creek from The Bund. At the end of 1843, when foreign trade first began at the port, there were only twenty-five foreigners in Shanghai, including officials and missionaries. In five years, the number of foreign residents had increased to 100, eighty-seven of whom were British. By 1855, there were 375 foreigners in the British Settlement. The 1865 census showed 460 foreigners in the French Concession. Ten years later, this number was reduced to 176, comprising twenty-one traders, 132 missionaries, and twenty-three civil servants and others.

A profile of the foreign population in the International Settlement by nationality that year showed that there were

2,297 residents and about the same number of military and naval personnel. After 1880, there was a general increase in Shanghai's foreign population, but the numbers were still small. By the end of the century, the number of foreigners, including the Japanese, reached only the thousands. Their numbers surged after 1900, largely due to Japanese and Russian immigration, until there were almost 100,000 foreigners in Shanghai by 1930.

From 1865 to 1935, for which reliable census statistics are available, nationals of forty-six countries lived in Shanghai's foreign settlements, but the majority of these nations were represented by no more than a handful of people. Until 1915, there were more Britons than any other foreign national group in Shanghai. After that year, there was still a substantial number of both British and Japanese residents, but the number of Japanese had surpassed the British.

The Japanese had been interested in Shanghai since 1880 when a ship was sent to survey the harbour, but it was not until after 1895, when Japan won the first Sino-Japanese War, that they obtained the same rights and privileges in China as other treaty powers. They opened mines and banks, built railways and factories, and became entrenched in Shanghai at Hongkew. Steadily, the Japanese became a formidable force in the city; one represented on the Municipal Council and backed by a military and naval presence.

Despite their small number, Americans had exerted a strong influence in Shanghai since the early days of foreign settlement. Early American traders sold opium under the umbrella of British firms since their own treaty agreement with the Chinese Empire had prohibited United States nationals from handling this contraband item. The number of American residents in Shanghai rose from 378 in

1865 to 1,608 in 1930, with the largest increase from 562 in 1900 to 911 in 1905. They worked closely with the British in organizing the International Settlement, and a member of the American firm, Russell & Company, always had a seat on the Municipal Council. American missionaries founded and controlled a number of secondary and tertiary educational institutions. The sons and daughters of prosperous Shanghai families might continue their tertiary education at St John's, or a missionary college in another Chinese city, or be sent abroad to study at universities in Britain, France, or the United States.

The number of Russian residents jumped from twenty-eight in 1895 to forty-seven in 1900 to 354 in 1905. The Bolshevik Revolution in 1917 and ensuing civil war brought more Russians to Shanghai. In 1920, there were 1,266 Russian in the city, in 1925 there were 2,766, and, by 1930, 3,487. Trained specialists were able to continue their professions, such as medicine and music. Others, skilled craftsmen and business managers, also found a demand for their services. Still more, especially members of the aristocracy with no professional know-how, had to earn a living any way they could. Some found jobs as bodyguards to rich Shanghaiese who were potential candidates for kidnapping, while others joined the police force. Many single women had to resort to becoming entertainers, hostesses in dancehalls, or prostitutes in order to make a living.

The presence of Indians in Shanghai was first recorded in 1880, when there were four, and in 1885, there were fifty-eight. The subsequent rises in the Indian population can be attributed to the number of Sikh policemen in the International Settlement. There had been Indian soldiers with the British in Shanghai since 1860, but it was not until 1884 that Indians began to serve in the police force.

Although Sikh policemen performed myriad law enforce-ment duties, they were most popularly portrayed directing traffic at busy street crossings. Their official red turban caused the Chinese to call them 'red-headed flies' or 'red-headed rascals'.

The foreign settlements were isolated from the Chinese population around them at the beginning, but the fourteen year Taiping Rebellion which began in 1850, and had established a capital in Nanking (Nanjing) by 1853, brought many Chinese refugees into the foreign settlements. Others subsequently followed for economic and political reasons. From almost every province Shanghai attracted men and women who sought a new chance in life. Kiangsu (Jiangsu), Chekiang (Zhejiang), Kwangtung, and Anhwei (Anhui) especially saw thousands of their people emigrate to Shanghai. Out of 620,421 Chinese living in the International Settlement in 1915, more than 75 percent, or 491,890 persons, had originally hailed from these four provinces.

The depression in the silk trade had brought skilled workers to Shanghai's textile mills from the traditional centres of sericulture, Hangchow (Hangzhou) in Chekiang and Soochow and Wusih (Wuxi) in Kiangsu. From Kwangtung came merchants and others experienced in foreign trade, especially those who had handled tea. Immigrants from Kiangsu, Anhui, and Chekiang provided the general labour force; many from Shantung (Shandong) joined the Settlement police. A survey by the Imperial Customs Service during the early part of the twentieth century found that the most popular restaurants in Shanghai boasted Cantonese cooks. The sons of Ningpo (Ningbo) in Chekiang had replaced the Cantonese as compradores. They also became seamen, carpenters, tailors, male laundry workers, store clerks, and members of the underworld gangs.

15

The basic law of the International Settlement was the Land Regulations. The Municipal Council, elected by the Ratepayers' Meeting, enjoyed legislative and administrative powers, control over taxation, finance, the police and security, as well as other routine responsibilities of municipal administration. It only needed to consult the Chinese authorities and foreign consuls in Shanghai, and representatives of the treaty powers in Peking, from time to time on certain constitutional issues. In making policies for the Settlement, the Municipal Council reflected the interests of groups that dominated it. Whereas the French government favoured their own nationals in the French Concession, the British allowed all nationalities to live and work in the International Settlement. How loud a voice each resident was permitted depended on the amount of property he possessed.

Stringent property qualifications for franchise in the International Settlement meant that both the Ratepayers' Meeting and the Municipal Council were dominated by moneyed interests. It was never a case of one person, one vote. Firms and individuals with several domiciles commanded a multiple number of votes. Among 669 ratepayers who attended the annual meeting of the ratepayers in 1935, fifteen of them controlled 136 out of a total of 897 votes (Fig. 2.1).

The British dominated all aspects of International Settlement life. The number of British firms and British voters surpassed all others throughout the history of the Settlement. In 1906, out of a total foreign male population of 5,728, only 1,597, or about 28 per cent, had the right to vote; and 960, or 17 per cent, were eligible for seats on the Municipal Council. More than half of the franchise-holders, 885 in total, were British. Not surprisingly, the British controlled

2.1 William R. Poate, President of the Shanghai Municipal Council, arrives for a meeting accompanied by his wife, *c.* 1900s.

the Municipal Council. Six or seven of the nine members were usually British. Major trading houses such as Jardine Matheson, Dent & Company, Butterfield and Swire, and the British banks, were always represented. There was usually one American representative and one missionary. Japanese interests were represented on the Council from 1902 but, the franchise was not extended to Chinese ratepayers who otherwise would have qualified as voters until the 1920s. The first Chinese Municipal Councillor took his seat in 1928.

The principle of extraterritoriality applied in Shanghai meant that foreign nationals were subject to the laws of their own countries and the jurisdiction of their own consuls. Chinese living in the International Settlement had to abide by Settlement laws. For them there was the Mixed Court for both civil and criminal cases, presided over by a Chinese magistrate appointed by the intendant, the Chinese local administrative official. In cases where a foreigner was a plaintiff, his government's consul at Shanghai would attend court as an assessor.

Taking advantage of the absence of Chinese authorities, radical intellectuals and students alike thrived in Shanghai's foreign settlements. Their newspapers and periodicals espousing revolutionary causes against the Ch'ing dynasty, however, made settlement authorities uneasy, particularly in the early years of the twentieth century. In one shop located on the ground floor of one of the many brothels on Foochow Road, books and political tracts entitled *Blood of Liberty* and *Pen of Revolution*, were displayed amidst pornographic publications such as *Timetable for Women*. Dissident writers and political activists became ever more active during the 1920s and 1930s, with the first meeting of revolutionaries that founded the Chinese Communist Party in 1921 taking place in the French Concession.

The French Concession was organized in 1849. Under the control of the French government from the outset through their minister at Peking and consul at Shanghai, the French community decided not to amalgamate with the other foreign-controlled areas when they were merged in 1863. At that time, the French community in Shanghai was concerned that, being small, it would be overwhelmed by the British; not an unjustifiable fear. Specific and irreconcilable issues, for instance, included such seemingly minor ones as the injunction against building wharfs along The Bund. The French traders felt that they could not afford the luxury of not using every inch of the river bank since the waterfront in the French Concession was so limited, whereas wharves in the International Settlement could be built along the Whangpoo north of Soochow Creek.

Furthermore, French nationals did not want to give up the preferential treatment they were enjoying in their own concession. French Catholic missionaries did not want to come under the constraints of the Protestant institutions that dominated settlement life.

As a result, the French Concession had its own Ratepayers' Meeting and Conseil municipal, but the French consul at Shanghai held certain additional and important powers. No meeting of ratepayers could take place without being called by the consul. He served as *ex-officio* chairman of the Conseil municipal and enjoyed the right to veto measures agreed by the Conseil. He also selected the items to be included in the budget for approval by the French minister at Peking. As chief executive and administrator, the consul appointed and dismissed employees of the Concession government, and retained control over the police. Even more importantly, he had the right to dissolve the Conseil and to declare martial law in times of emergency.

In China, clan elders played an important role in village disputes. In the absence of such a traditional social structure in Shanghai's foreign settlements, other forces took over. The underworld syndicates, the most prominent being the Green Gang, moved into the French Concession during the Taiping Rebellion. This gang owed its origin to the organisation of tribute grain transport coolies on the Grand Canal and, in Shanghai, gained control of labourers from rickshaw coolies to factory workers. Most powerful during the 1920s and 1930s, the Green Gang was led by a triumvirate of leaders: Huang Ching-yung (Huang Jingrong), Tu Yueh-sheng (Du Yuesheng), and Chang Hsiao-lin (Zhang Xiaolin). They, and others, also controlled the opium traffic, vice establishments, as well as the protection rackets. Gang leaders came to hold positions comparable to that of clan or village elders in traditional Chinese communities. Huang was actually the chief of detectives in the French Concession police force. Tu, who dominated the gang after 1927, wielded tremendous influence in all aspects of life in Shanghai. He was elected to seats on the Conseil municipal, the Stock Exchange, and the boards of various financial and charitable institutions.

From 1843 to the end of the nineteenth century, the Chinese administration in the old city remained substantially unchanged. The local administrative official was the intendant, who dealt directly with the foreign consuls. Originally, he was assigned by the imperial government to oversee foreign trade and the collection of customs revenues in Shanghai, but step-by-step foreign consuls and Settlement authorities assumed responsibilities for trade regulations. When the Small Knife rebels destroyed the Customs House in 1853, the Inspectorate of Imperial Customs, formed under foreign control with a Briton permanently as Inspector General, also took away the right to collect customs duties from the Chinese local administration. The Boxer Protocol, signed in 1901 after China was defeated by the combined international force after the Boxer Rebellion, removed all remaining duties from foreign goods, further lessening the power and prestige of the Chinese imperial government.

Amid the decline of Chinese imperial power during the last decades of the nineteenth century and the early years of the twentieth, China's commerce, industry, and mining developed, enhancing the growth of the treaty ports. Many of these new ventures established their bases of operation in Shanghai. The demand for capital and labour brought into the city a large number of Chinese entrepreneurs as well as peasant labourers. These enterprising men, together with many foreign traders and adventurers,—all living and working in the foreign settlements—enabled Shanghai to become one of the most colourful cities of all time.

3

Shanghai at Work: Commerce, Industry, and Finance

THE principal reason behind the British decision to establish a settlement in Shanghai was its desire to trade with the Chinese Empire but, in time, Shanghai was also to develop into a financial and industrial centre of international renown.

By 1853, ten years after opening to foreign trade, the city had surpassed all other Chinese ports, including Canton, in the amount of goods shipped. Throughout the century that foreign privileges remained in China, Shanghai maintained its status as the leading Chinese port in foreign and related domestic trade. Goods from overseas as well as the Chinese hinterland were gathered in Shanghai, then shipped to their destinations. Internally, goods were shipped from Shanghai to the Yangtze River ports as well as those along the Grand Canal, and, by road and railway as well, as these facilities were constructed. Internationally, ships sailed from and to Europe, the Americas, Africa, and all ports in Asia (Fig. 3.1). In 1932, shipping totalling 34,017,467 tonnes carried imports and exports through the port of Shanghai valued at 827,788,000 Haikwan (Customs) taels, at that time worth roughly thirty million pounds sterling.

The first foreign trading companies in Shanghai were predominantly British, organized in a traditional British manner as branch offices of major houses already established at Canton and Hong Kong. This pattern was adopted by other foreign companies, and, to a certain extent, by modern Chinese companies as well. Management was synonymous with investment, so partners or members of the major

3.1 The bustling Whangpoo waterfront in 1928. To the left is Pootung; on the right the French Concession.

owner's family headed both the main and branch offices. Partners in Shanghai, therefore, enjoyed a great deal of autonomy, but they had to consult the head office on certain matters, especially those concerning money.

Two major British companies that have survived the test of time are Jardine, Matheson & Company (Fig. 3.2), and Butterfield and Swire (Fig. 3.3). The former had begun trading with China even before the Opium War of 1840. By the second decade of the twentieth century, companies owned by Jardine Matheson in Shanghai had given up the opium trade altogether, and turned to silk filature, cotton spinning and weaving, timber, packing and storage, and the ownership of at least one brewery. Butterfield and Swire (Taikoo) started as a business in the transportation of goods in China by opening an office in Shanghai in 1867. It also operated

3.2 The Shanghai headquarters of Jardine, Matheson & Company.

3.3
Butterfield and Swire based their Shanghai office in this building from 1908 to 1954.

the China Navigation Company for inland and coastal trade, and the Taikoo Dockyard in Hong Kong (Fig. 3.3).

A company's successes and failures in China depended greatly on the skills, judgement and personality of the partner in Shanghai, as well as his ability to get along with people. The actual buying and selling was handled by Chinese compradores who worked directly with the partners. The first Shanghai compradores were Cantonese, and many of them were partners in the companies that employed them; even more were independent businessmen in their own right (Fig. 3.4).

3.4 A group of the marketing staff of Butterfield and Swire, Shanghai. The Chinese men were comparadores.

Beneath the partners, the operation of a trading company was usually divided into six major departments, reflecting the nature of the merchandise handled. These were most likely to be the export of silk and tea, and the import of 'Manchester goods' (mostly cotton piece goods), shipping and insurance, land and housing agency, and 'muck and truck'. 'Muck and truck' comprised such export goods as hides, horsehair, leather, bristles, and art objects, and import goods such as cotton yarn, hardware, and machinery. Opium was handled by the partner and his chief compradore in Shanghai, so did not show up on the company's organization chart. After the 1890s, those companies which had prospered diversified into other areas such as manufacturing and mining.

Before the 1880s, the bread and butter of Shanghai's foreign trade was the export of tea and silk, and the import of opium. Until 1858, when the opium trade was legalized, ships bringing opium from India stopped at Woosung in order to avoid the consuls at the treaty ports. The British government did not openly support the trade, but private companies, including leading trading houses in Hong Kong and Shanghai, were involved. After 1858, David Sassoon and Sons gained control of the trade through manipulating the opium supply in Bombay.

Beginning in the 1850s, the Taiping Rebellion disrupted the old tea and silk routes to Canton, so Shanghai and Foochow (Fuzhou) became centres for the tea trade. The tea trading season was April and May, when leaves were ripening on the hillside. The trading houses in Shanghai would send compradores into the tea production areas of Chiukiang (Jiujiang), Hankow (Hankou), and Hangchow to make purchases. Tea procurement was highly competitive, and it was the companies with large opium stocks that were able to exploit the tea market most successfully by paying for their purchases of tea with opium. The less successful firms eventually resorted to smuggling young plants out of China to India and Ceylon, where conditions were favourable for tea gardens. As a result, tea exports declined after 1880 as plants in India and Ceylon matured. Whereas

25

ninety-seven per cent of the tea imported into Britain had come from China in 1869, only twenty per cent was from China by 1898, and a mere three per cent by 1902.

The silk-trading season more or less coincided with the tea season. Trading firms in Shanghai sent their compradores to the silk producing areas of Wusih, Soochow, and Hangchow, but Chinese silk-traders themselves brought their wares to Shanghai for inspection by foreign experts. In 1857, 80,000 bales of silk, valued at 21,700,000 silver dollars, were exported from Shanghai. The year 1870 proved to be a notable one for Chinese silk for two reasons. The completion of the Suez Canal had shortened the distance between China and Europe by half, and a silk-worm disease had completely destroyed the silk production in France and Italy. Hence the demand for Chinese silk rose, but in the long run competition from Japan for the international silk market proved to be too strong, and after 1880 China's share of the international market began to decline.

During the final decades of the nineteenth century, modern manufacturing facilities began to be built in the treaty ports, producing goods for sale in China as well as for export. Manufacturers in Shanghai concentrated on light industries. Despite Chinese government efforts to establish a shipyard and an arsenal in Shanghai, by far the largest industrial sector was textiles, comprising cotton spinning and weaving, silk reeling, wool spinning and weaving, dyeing and printing designs onto finished materials, and garment knitting and manufacturing. In addition there was production of food and related items, including flour milling, medicine, matches, paper, glass. Railways and steamships made the transportation of raw materials and finished products easier and cheaper.

Tobacco and egg products came next in importance. The

tobacco industry consisted principally of cigarette rolling, using mostly domestic tobacco after the 1890s. Earlier efforts at cigarette manufacture had been to no avail as Chinese smokers could not be enticed away from ingesting tobacco through the water pipe. It was the Americans who first brought modern cigarette rolling to Shanghai. A merging with British interests to form the British-American Tobacco Company of China followed in 1902, and thus factories elsewhere in China were also established. Advertising and sales campaigns were carried out all over China, including the remote areas of the north-west, to promote cigarette smoking.

One effect of a concentration of manufacturing in Shanghai was the increase in the number of industrial workers, leading to the development of a labour union movement. By the 1930s there were 75,242 workers in 567 factories in the International Settlement, and 73,448 in 690 factories in the Chinese municipality of Shanghai, which was established by the Nationalist government after 1927. A little more than half of the city's labour force was employed in textiles, producing 40 to 60 per cent of the value of industrial output. In 1937, an estimated 200,000 workers were employed in the cotton textile factories of Shanghai; a ready-made urban proletariat for political organizers. In 1924, the Shanghai Federation of Labour Unions, embracing forty unions and 40,000 workers, tended to support the Nationalists. One year later, it was definitely under the control of the Communists as, within this one year, union membership had risen to 200,000 with new members supporting the Communist cause. This development was one of the reasons why the Green Gang leaders, accustomed to controlling the industrial work force, joined forces with Chiang Kai-shek and the Nationalists in 1927 in the blood bath which crushed the Communist attempt to take-over Shanghai.

As an ever increasing need arose to finance its multi-faceted trade and manufacturing enterprises, Shanghai became a banking centre. When imperialist rivalry among Western countries intensified, each nation with aspirations in China opened banks in Shanghai. These foreign banks principally financed the import and export trade of their own nationals, while some also served as agents for their governments; work which entailed receiving deposits of Chinese Maritime Customs duty and salt gabelle pledged against government loans.

British banks dominated the financial services of the port. The first British bank to survive the test of time was the Chartered Bank of India, Australia and China with headquarters in London. The Shanghai branch opened in 1857, but traders in China frequently found the Chartered Bank to be less than immediately responsive to their demands. It was not until 1865, when the Hongkong and Shanghai Bank established a branch in Shanghai, that local British traders had a bank that catered to their particular needs.

American interests were represented by the foreign banking arm of the First National Bank of New York City, which opened the first American bank in Shanghai in 1902. The Chase Bank brought its operations to Shanghai in 1920 as the Equitable Eastern Banking Corporation, changing its name to the Chase National Bank in 1931. The Netherlands Trading Society, a Dutch bank, opened a Shanghai branch in 1903, and the Deutsche-Asiatische Bank was established in 1889. The Yokohama Specie Bank opened in 1892 to finance Japanese trade and manufacturing. In 1895, the Russo-Chinese Bank was founded to finance the construction of the Chinese Eastern Railway in Manchuria. The

French brought the Banque de l'Indochine to Shanghai in 1899. The Bank of Taiwan, an official-private joint banking venture, opened by the Japanese after the Sino-Japanese War in Taiwan, established a branch in Shanghai in April 1911 (Fig. 3.5).

None of the foreign banks achieved the power and influence

3.5 Foreign banks on the Bund, 1928.

of the Hongkong and Shanghai Banking Corporation, which in 1923 moved its Shanghai headquarters into an imposing building on The Bund designed by the architectural firm of Palmer and Turner which was well-established in both ports. Controlled by local British traders in Hong Kong and Shanghai, the bank enjoyed a virtual monopoly over the financing of foreign trade in China for more than two decades. Its growth during the first decade was spectacular because the British dominated foreign trade and controlled the Chinese Imperial Customs, while the staff of the bank got along well with the traders and civil servants of Shanghai. From the 1890s onwards, the bank's growth was further enhanced by considerable underwriting of the borrowing of the Chinese government and the expansion of the railways. As a guarantee for such bonds, Chinese government revenue and a large percentage of other taxes were deposited with this bank.

Towards the end of the nineteenth century, old-style traditional Chinese financial institutions, the money shops, worked alongside Western-style modern banks. Attempts by Chinese merchants who traded with foreigners and compradores of foreign firms in Shanghai to establish modern banks began during the 1860s, but these ventures were not successful. The first Chinese-owned modern bank in Shanghai, the Imperial Bank of China, was opened in May 1897. The Bank of China, recapitalized by the Nationalist government in 1927, had its beginning as the Great Ch'ing Bank in 1905. Other Chinese-owned banks established before the fall of the Ch'ing dynasty in 1911 included the Bank of Communications in 1907 and the Chekiang Industrial Bank, also founded in 1907. After 1912, there was a burst of public and private banking activities in Shanghai. The Shanghai Commercial Savings Bank was established by K. P. Chen (1881–1976). The 1926 issue of the Banking Year Book listed 390 banking institutions in China, but by 1935, there were as many as seventy-three branches of domestic banks with head offices outside Shanghai, and 101 branches of thirty-five banks with head offices in Shanghai.

By the 1930s, Shanghai was listed with London, Paris, Rome, Bombay, Tokyo, Chicago, and New York among the world's most cosmopolitan cities. In 1934, it was the busiest international port in Asia, and China's gateway to the world.

4

Shanghai Lifestyles

THE Chinese and foreign residents of Shanghai might mingle at work when it was mutually beneficial, but almost invariably they spent their leisure hours separately.

There was no actual segregation of nationalities or races, but there were national clubs such as the French Club and the American Club; the latter the first to open to Chinese membership. Public parks in Shanghai were not open to the Chinese, ostensibly to keep out the less attractive elements of the population and to avoid crowding. It was said that since the Chinese had parks of their own there was no reason for them to crowd into parks frequented by foreign residents. Eventually attitudes changed, and after the Ratepayers' Meeting passed a resolution in June 1928, 'Jessfield and Hongkew Parks, the Public Gardens, the Bund Lawns and Foreshore, Quisan Gardens, and Brenan Piece (were) opened to the Chinese on the same terms as foreigners.' Far from taking umbrage, the Shanghai Chinese responded to this new state of affairs with great enthusiasm and in good humour (Fig. 4.1).

In the early days of the settlements, the non-Chinese staff of foreign owned companies in Shanghai consisted mainly of single young men who lived in company quarters and dined in the company mess. Before fifty years had passed, however, the leisure hours of well-heeled foreign residents were already well organized. Weekend excursions to nearby sites of interest, such as Soochow or Hangchow, reachable by boat via the Grand Canal or Lake T'ai (Tai) often took place. Hunters did not have far to go in search of game. On the lakes and ponds to the west of Shanghai, there was mandarin duck, and in the nearby hills, pheasant, deer, wild pig, hare, and partridge. The

4.1
Mr and Mrs C. C. Chao, parents of Hong Kong resident Raymond Chao, enjoy a visit to Jessfield Park in 1938.

North China Daily News jubilee edition records a 'big bag' by a group of hunters from Shanghai between 10 December to Christmas Day 1893: '1,629 head, made up of seventy-four deer, 1,497 pheasants, forty-seven duck and teal, and eleven extras.' Wild boar and wild pig were discovered to be 'excellent specimen of the species.' Several heads were mounted by taxidermists for the Shanghai Museum of Natural History.

Not long after the opening of the port, families joined the foreign residents of Shanghai. In the days of the horse and carriage and later when cars came into vogue, foreign ladies would be driven along Bubbling Well Road. The majority played bridge, took part in amateur dramatics, sang in choirs, worked with charitable organizations, and went shopping. They also attended sports functions as spectators rather than participants but, as the twentieth century arrived, they began to play tennis. Their daughters went to dancing schools as well as regular schools for foreign female children, such as the Cathedral School for Girls on Yates Road (Fig. 4.2). Shanghai can even claim that the late Dame Margot Fonteyn, born Peggy Hookum in the city, began her ballet studies there. Young ladies made their débuts at balls or receptions held at such places as the French Club, then graduated to tea dances in one of the socially acceptable hotels, such as the Astor House overlooking Soochow Creek. Marriage, preferably with one of the eligible young businessmen in Shanghai, usually followed (Figs. 4.3, 4.4).

4.2 Students at the Cathedral School for Girls give a performance at the conclusion of the 1930 school year.

4.3
The Astor House Hotel, owned by Ezra and Kadoorie interests, stood in three acres of grounds close to the Bund across Garden Bridge.

4.4 Claire Kammerling, daughter of a manager of the Astor House Hotel, celebrated her sixteenth birthday there in 1930.

The male offspring led more adventurous lives. From an early age, they followed their fathers and uncles into places such as brothels and gaming houses which were forbidden to their mothers, sisters, female cousins, and aunts. Whereas sons of missionaries were sent home to boarding-schools and universities, few businessmen sent their children to spend much of their youth being educated abroad. Academic training beyond what the Shanghai Public School had to offer was not normally considered necessary for the scions who were destined to take on the responsibilities of running large business enterprises in Asia.

Much leisure time was spent in the many social and sporting clubs where one could swim and sail, play tennis, cricket, golf, football, rugby, polo, baseball, lawn bowling, and field hockey. Membership of the Shanghai Race Club was a significant status symbol (Fig. 4.5). Racing and riding had been popular since the early days of the settlement, with the first recorded race in April 1848, but

1. Ye-tsun Tsur, second right, President of Tsinghua University in Peking and formerly at St John's, with his family. Tsur's children received higher education in China or abroad. One son graduated from St John's, Shanghai; a daughter is a 1939 graduate of Bryn Mawr College, USA.

2. Wah Sam, the Shanghai compradore of the Hongkong and Shanghai Banking Corporation, was 37 when this photograph was taken in 1874.

3. Single-wheeled carts were a popular means of transport in China for both goods and people. In Shanghai they were used well into the twentieth century.

4. The Shanghai waterfront viewed across the Whangpoo River from Pootung. Oil painting by an unknown Chinese artist, *c.* 1840s.

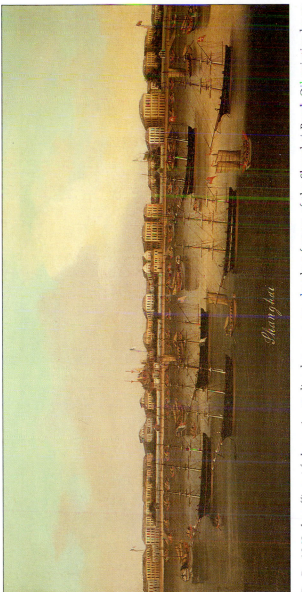

Shanghai

5. By 1849 the offices of the major trading houses were already a feature of the Shanghai Bund. Oil painting by an unknown Chinese artist, 1849.

6. Water-colour of the Shanghai waterfront office of the Hongkong and Shanghai Banking Corporation prepared by its architects, Palmer & Turner, 1923.

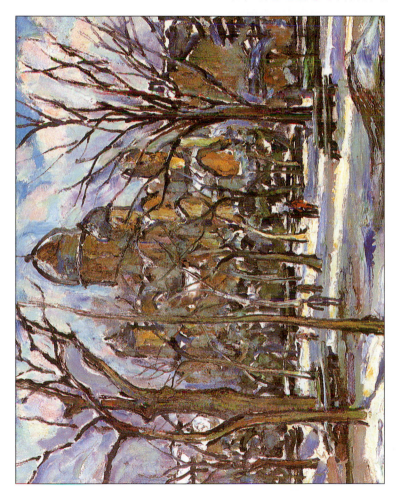

7. Painting in Western media flourished in Old Shanghai. Here, a contemporary Shanghai artist, Chen Jun De, has depicted Xiang Yang Park (formerly the French Park) in Impressionist style in oil, 1988.

8. Located at the junction of the Whangpoo River and Soochow Creek, the Russian consulate was recently returned to its original owners by the Shanghai government.

9. A pavilion in the Yu Yuan, a garden built by a Ming dynasty official in the old Chinese city.

10. A garden adjacent to the thirteenth-century Confucian temple at Chia-ting, now a suburb of metropolitan Shanghai.

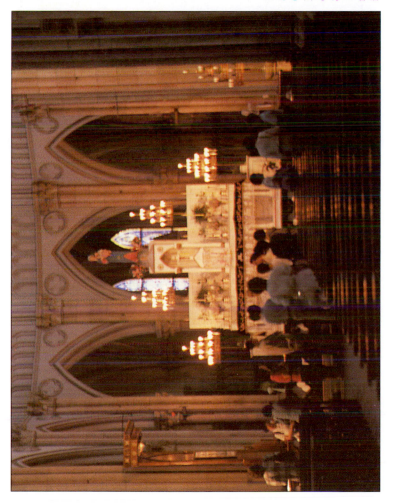

11. The interior of St Ignatius Cathedral, the Roman Catholic cathedral at Siccawei built in 1906. Services recommenced there in 1979.

12. Three and four storey buildings of Old Shanghai close to Garden Bridge.

13. The Bund today, with the former Shanghai Club in the left foreground.

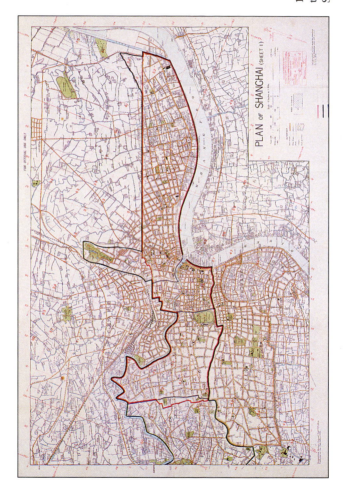

14. A street plan of the International Settlement in 1935.

15. The Grand Canal, completed in the seventh century to link northern China to the rice producing Yangtze Delta, is reached from Shanghai via Soochow Creek.

16. Throughout the more than 700 years of Shanghai's existence as a centre of domestic and international trade, the confluence of the Whangpoo River and Soochow Creek has been an important river traffic junction.

4.5 The Shanghai Race Club in 1928. The race-course itself is in the background on the left.

horse-racing had been regularly taking place since 1846. Racing in Shanghai was confined to China ponies, which were brought from the north of the country, then trained in Shanghai. Sometimes visiting naval vessels provided the opportunity for special social events and religious services, such as the Easter morning service in 1930 abroad the USS *Pittsburgh* (Fig. 4.6). Scouting was active, as were service clubs such as the Rotarians.

Not all expatriate residents could boast an extravagant lifestyle, but, several general conclusions can be made about the basic lifestyle of foreigners in Shanghai. Expenditure on household items such as food was higher than that of the Chinese but, except for the very wealthy Chinese, the foreign residents lived more comfortably and spaciously. The 14 September 1850 issue of the *North-China Herald* noted that market prices in the

4.6 Easter morning service on board the USS *Pittsburgh*, Shanghai, 1930.

British Settlement and Chinese city showed a difference of 25 cents per catty for chicken, while eggs were 6 cents each for foreigners, but 40 cents per 100 in the Chinese market.

Communication between the Chinese and foreigners who did not speak the other's language was pidgin English. It was a truly colourful language that was comprehensible only to its devotees. Pidgin-English speakers fitted English words, or what were thought to be the proper English expressions, into what was considered to be a Chinese grammatical framework, and prayed that the result made sense. 'Here', referring to location, was 'this side' in pidgin, while 'there' was 'that side'. 'Come at once!' was 'Come chop chop!' Of course, this form of speech was shunned by respectable Chinese craftsmen, who used their own version of the King's English in their daily dealings with foreigners. At a well-patronized tailoring shop on Nanking Road, there was a prominently displayed sign that told all who entered what to do: 'Ladies have fits upstairs'.

As a rule, the lifestyle of the wealthy Chinese was ostentatious. They built western-style houses in the foreign settlements as these had the modern amenities and paraphernalia which symbolised their wealth. Hsu Jun (Xu Run) (1838–1911), known alternatively as Ahyune or Ayun, for example, compradore of Dent & Company in Shanghai, lived in the International Settlement in a foreign-style residence with a grand garden. 'Eighteen servants kept the place spic and span', observed a foreign woman who had been a guest, 'the house was so clean that its floors and desks were as shining as glass'. When Hsu went bankrupt, he placed his affairs in the hands of the twenty-two money shops which were his principal creditors.

4.7 A Shanghai street in 1919; one which well illustrates the intermingling of Chinese and Western influences.

Others Chinese residents, not so wealthy but comfortably well-off, lived in one-family dwellings or apartment houses among the foreigners in the International Settlement or the French Concession (Fig. 4.7). Many, businessmen or professionals, were educated in Western-style schools in Shanghai where the teaching was in English or French, and then went on to a prestigious local university, such as St John's, where a network could be cemented for future business and social relationships. Those who could went abroad for tertiary and post-graduate studies, and returned to good jobs in Shanghai's commercial and financial institutions (Fig. 4.8). They married spouses of their own rather than their parents' choice, and adopted many modern lifestyle habits and customs, including the Christian faith. They kept certain traditional Chinese habits, nevertheless, such as large households. But no matter how Westernized a Chinese household became it never gave up Chinese cuisine. Food was expensive since it had to be imported from outside the area, and vegetables had to be preserved to last all winter, but, in general, the Shanghaiese dined well (Fig. 4.9).

4.8 Mrs Chu's seventieth birthday party in 1937. The family was prominent in Shanghai and, in a dark gown at the front, is Samuel Chu, who later became Managing Director of Jardine Insurance in Hong Kong.

4.9
As winter approaches,
Lee-Chung Kung and
her brother Edward,
children of S.W. Kung,
a Shanghai banker,
pose on the roof of
their house in
Bubbling Well Road,
c. 1937.

A general knowledge of Western civilization as well as Western-style education were first introduced to China in Shanghai. Missionaries expanded their proselyting activities to embrace the dissemination of more general information. Works of literature, politics and economics, as well as science and technology, were translated into Chinese. Current affairs also became a focus of interest. In addition to St John's, which was founded in 1879, Aurora University was established by the Jesuits in 1903. The Chinese themselves established Jiao Tong University in 1896 and Tung Chi (Tong Ji) University in 1907. John Dewey visited Shanghai in 1919 and Bertrand Russell in 1920, both leaving behind a large body of adherents. There were academies specialising in art, music, drama, and science. The creation of these varied institutions made Shanghai the centre of new learning in China.

Libraries and museums were an integral part of Old Shanghai. The Museum of Natural History came into being in 1868 when the French missionary and naturalist, Père Pierre Heude (1836–1902) gave his collection for exhibition in Shanghai in a specially built museum. Père Heude was a botanist as well as a zoologist, and his collection, which included specimens gathered in China, the Philippines, Indo-China, and Malaya, was noted especially for the flora and fauna of the Yangtze region. The Shanghai Museum, housing a collection of works of art and artifacts, was opened in 1874. The Municipal Council at first funded this museum with a grant of 250 taels in 1877, then raised it to 500 taels in 1878 and 1879. In 1907, the grant was 1,000 taels. From the outset, the museum enjoyed the services of professional curators and was thus able to maintain an extremely high standard. As a result, it has always received support from learned societies and museums abroad, particularly those in Britain and the United States.

The new lifestyle prompted the Shanghai Chinese to organize Western-style social and sporting clubs of their own—the Kiangwan (Jiangwan) Race Club for example—but, even so, the majority preferred to stay with traditional leisure activities. Although they might learn the intricacies of bridge and billiards, mahjongg remained the favourite table game. The Temple of the City God and the Bubbling Well Temple attracted large crowds during certain festival seasons. Shops, restaurants, theatres, and myriad other forms of entertainment were found in the foreign settlements.

Shanghai's men danced in ballrooms with professional host-esses as well as young women who considered themselves 'modern'; and they danced to the latest tune popular in New York or Paris, or listened to jazz into the small hours of the night. At the same time, they enjoyed various gen-res of the Chinese opera; the most popular being Kunshan opera performed by amateur troupes.

Tea-houses, some of which featured instrumental music and melodic recitations, were in most cases just innocent places for doing business and meeting friends. Other estab-lishments were responsible for Shanghai gaining a inter-national reputation as a notorius den of iniquity. Opium, gambling, and prostitution were connected, and all under the control of the underworld leaders. No 181 Avenue Foch, opened in 1927 in the French Concession, was the domi-cile of 'China's greatest gambling-house'. The monthly rental for this establishment, occuping one entire city block, was said to be 4,000 Chinese dollars. Gambling possibil-ities included roulette, black jack, and mahjongg; food and women were also part of the offerings of the house. These grand establishments were restricted to members, while others, less glamorous, were patronized by Chinese and non-Chinese residents, tourists, or sailors on shore leave.

Shanghai's Chinese population flocked to the large-scale entertainment complexes established from the 1920s. Such 'palaces' offered a variety of amusements, which combined traditional performing arts with modern ways of having fun. There was Shanghai opera, Shao-hsing (Shaoxing) opera, Soochow recitations, Peking opera, modern cinemas, and, in one case, even an ice-skating rink. Stalls sold all man-ner of fast food which was popular with crowds who had not come to spend time sitting at restaurant tables. The New World at the corner of Nanking Road and Tibet Road pioneered this kind of entertainment. Doors opened at two in the afternoon and did not close until the small hours. Its rival in the French Concession, the Great World, came under the control of the leaders of the Green Gang when the original investors began to lose money.

The Shanghai Chinese also discovered American cinema with a vengeance. At first, newsreels were shown in make-shift open-air theatres during summer evenings, such as the one created in 1924 in the garden of the St George's Hotel on Bubbling Well Road. Competition was keen, however, and the popularity of this theatre did not survive beyond a year. By 1925, most customers had moved to the Italian Garden on Garden Road. Gradually, as feature length films became available, and especially when those made in Shanghai became successful, indoor theatres such as the Majestic were built (Fig. 4.10). A film industry began in China after the techniques of cinematography were commercialized by film makers in Shanghai. There were travelogues, and full-length features dealing with social problems of traditional ethics and morality where the line between good and evil was simply drawn and forcefully presented. Actresses such as Juan Lingyü (Ruan Lingyu) and Butterfly (Hu Tie) attracted a following comparable to the stars of Hollywood.

For the industrial labourers far outside the good life, Shanghai was a harsh environment because wages were low and working hours long. Male workers earned higher wages than women or children, with the result that except in ship-building, factory-workers were predominantly women and children. An 1899 survey showed that out of a labour force of 34,500 in forty-three factories, 20,000 were women and 7,000 children. A 1929 survey of 1,781 factories showed that there were 126,500 women workers, 76,500 adult male workers, and 20,650 children in Chapei and Pootung (Pudong).

4.10 The Majestic Theatre bedecked for a gala evening on 16 October 1941. The film featured was *Moon Over Miami* starring Don Ameche and Betty Grable.

In 1929, the highest daily wage of 1.75 dollars was earned by male workers in silk-weaving, and the lowest daily wage of 12 cents was earned by women in match factories. During the first decades of the twentieth century, workers in Shanghai went on strike thirty-six times, twenty-two of which were related to wage demands.

Young women were recruited for Shanghai's textile mills from their home villages in northern Kiangsu (Jiangsu). In many cases, the only place these lonely young women knew outside the mills was the Young Women's Christian Association (YWCA) where they could be taught how to read and write. Cora Deng, a graduate of the missionary Ginling College in Nanking who had discovered dialectic materialism while studying at the London School of Economics, used the Marxist writings as her text when introducing social consciousness to her charges.

Conditions for those with even less income than factory labourers were grim indeed. The old city and the more settled areas outside were extremely crowded. The deterioration of sanitary conditions meant that cholera and other communicable diseases were common. Fire was also a major problem since charcoal and dried reeds were the principal sources of fuel for most of Chinese households, and the houses themselves were constructed of wood. Furthermore, a large number of families lived on the boats which crowded the Whangpoo waterfront and Soochow Creek; boats with low, arched bamboo mats as their only protection. The men worked as casual labourers and performed odd jobs on the wharfs, while the women added to the family earnings by stitching old rags together to make shoe soles; or mending torn garments for other wharf coolies who had no families. Their earnings were never more than a few cents at a time.

Deaths from exposure and starvation were frequent. In 1935, when the compulsory registration of births and deaths first became law in Shanghai, there were 5,725 entries under the category of 'exposed corpses'; human remains left on the streets or wharfs until charitable organizations took them away for burial.

Shanghai, therefore, like comparable cities in the Europe and America, had its own, and perhaps larger, share of economic and social problems beneath the surface glitter and sophistication.

5

A Backward Glimpse Into the Jewish Community

DESPITE being relatively small in number, the Jewish community played a significant role in Shanghai life. Among their many business activities, they were important landlords, for example. With few exceptions, they fell into three groups: the Sephardim, the Ashkenazim, and the group of Europeans dominated by German Jews.

The Sephardic Jews were by far the most prominent. Among the first foreign traders in Shanghai, and bearing such names as Sassoon, Kadoorie, Ezra, and Abraham, they were part of the contemporary international mercantile community, in addition to enjoying business and personal links with the close-knit Jewish communities in Hong Kong and Bombay. At first they traded in raw cotton and general goods; then they took over the opium trade. In time, in Shanghai as well as Hong Kong and Bombay, they branched out into real estate, banking, shipping, warehousing, insurance, hotels, utilities, and other industries. Thus power and influence were gained as is well illustrated by the discovery that the names of thirty-eight prominent Sephardic Jews were among the 1932 list of the ninety-nine members of the Shanghai Stock Exchange.

Immediately following the completion of the trans-Siberian railroad and the pogrom in 1905, Russian Jews moved to Manchuria, with about 300 filtering down to Shanghai. After the Bolshevik Revolution in 1917, more than 10,000 Jews emigrated to Harbin. In the mid-1920s when White Russian and Japanese interests began to spread in Manchuria, many of the earlier immigrants moved southward to Tientsin

(Tianjin) and Shanghai, swelling the total Jewish population in Shanghai to almost 2,000.

The Ashkenazi Jews in Shanghai, mostly Russian but by then joined by stragglers from Lithuania as well, increased to more than 1,000 in 1924. They were not exactly welcomed by the Sephardic community, since they were not princes of commerce, but small businessmen engaged in the importing and exporting of such items as wool, bristles, and fur or door-to-door salesmen hawking rugs and other items. There were also differences of emphasis in religious beliefs and rituals, but among the Ashkenazi Jews were professional men trained as physicians and lawyers, for instance, and above all, there were musicians, who became a dominating group in both the Shanghai Municipal Orchestra and night club bands.

German and Eastern European Jews came to Shanghai in the years following 1938 as a result of Nazi persecutions in Europe. Some who were not permitted to enter other countries came to Shanghai as it was the only port that accepted people without passports or visas. They travelled by water, or by the Siberian Railroad to Manchuria, then from there to Japan. The Japanese consul at Vilna in Poland, apparently for humanitarian reasons, issued transit visas for those who possessed another country's visa, usually a Latin American country, but for those who did not have any visa at all, the destination was to be Shanghai. Among this latter group were the rabbinical staff and student body of the Yeshiva of Poland, which meant that, until the school moved to New York City after 1945, rabbis were trained in Shanghai.

When the Sino-Japanese conflict merged into World War II on 8 December 1941, a Japanese occupation of the International Settlement took place. Jews living there were treated according to their nationalities; those with Allied nationalities were interned. The large refugee community, either with 'non-enemy alien' status or stateless, worked in the factories. In 1943, when special privileges enjoyed by foreigners in China came to an end as the unequal treaties of the nineteenth century were formally abrogated by agreement between China and the international powers, the Jewish population in Shanghai was estimated to number 25,000.

David Sassoon was the first Jewish trader in China. The Sassoons had been established in Baghdad for several generations by the time David Sassoon was born in 1793. Leaving Baghdad for Bombay in 1825 he organized a company to export raw cotton to China and Britain. At that time, the East India Company still maintained a monopoly on tea, but had adopted the practice permitting their staff deck space on company ships to carry private goods between India and China. Employees who later made names for themselves in Asia, like Jardine and Matheson, had used their allotted space to ship opium grown specifically in India for cash sale in China, despite the fact that it was banned by the Chinese authorities.

David Sassoon & Company, incorporated in London to buy and sell raw cotton, began to trade opium in the early 1830s. After the Opium War ended in 1842, the company moved into Hong Kong, and into Shanghai as soon as a British presence was established there. It was partly due to Sassoon's manipulation of the opium supply and the opium market that led Jardine, Matheson to abandon this commodity and diversify its interests in Hong Kong and China. After 1871, David Sassoon controlled the opium market but, nevertheless, the family had gained sufficient influence and power for his elder brother, Abdullah Sassoon, who had remained to supervise the family's business in Bombay, to become a member of the Bombay Legislative Council.

David Sassoon died in Bombay in 1864. He married twice, and had a number of sons who took turns in managing the offices in Hong Kong, Shanghai, and London. After David's death, his second son, Elias David Sassoon, established E. D. Sassoon & Company, and thereafter there were two Sassoon companies which became known by contemporaries as the Old Sassoon (David Sassoon & Company), and the New Sassoon (E. D. Sassoon & Company). A number of employees of Old Sassoon, such as Silas Hardoon, joined E. D. Sassoon & Company as partners.

Shortly after the arrival of the British consul at Shanghai in 1843, three young employees of David Sassoon & Company began working and living in Shanghai. These were E. J. Abraham, M. S. Moshee, and J. Reuben; the last a founder of the Jewish congregation, Sheerith Israel. They were quickly followed by other Jewish young men. At first, Sephardic men returned to Baghdad or Bombay for their brides, but eventually, as more Jewish families settled in Shanghai, marriage partners were chosen locally.

Despite being singled out by Cecil Roth in *The Sassoon Dynasty* as the one Jewish family of Shanghai closely associated with scholarship, the Abraham men were first of all merchants handling commodities typical of that time, including opium. Eleazer Abraham had come to China as a clerk in David Sassoon & Company. In 1843 he was in Hong Kong; by 1850 he was working in Shanghai. There is on record a law suit brought by E. D. J. Abraham against the Apcar Steamship Company, owned by the Sassoons, to recover opium that had been lost in transit.

The grandson of the first Abraham in Shanghai, R. D. Abraham, was chosen leader of the Jewish community, and served it well. His son, Ezekiel Abraham, recalled how the community had rallied to support the refugees from Eastern Europe and Germany in 1938 and 1941 when some 17,000 to 18,000 found their way to Shanghai. The Japanese comman-

der had called in R. D. Abraham, as leader of the Jewish community, to tell him that a shipload of Jewish refugees had
arrived. 'We cannot let them land,' said the Japanese. 'Why?'
Abraham wanted to know. 'There is no place for them to live,
and the refugees have no money to feed themselves', reasoned
the Japanese. 'In that case,' pronounced Abraham without a
smile, 'you will just have to shoot all of them, because there
is no other place on earth for them to go.' Then he paused for
a few moments before announcing, 'or, we can open the Sassoon
warehouses in Hongkew to house the refugees, and put them
to work in the factories.'

Edward Ezra was the first person born in Shanghai and educated at the Shanghai Public School to be elected to the Municipal
Council. By 1900 he had switched from the opium trade to
large-scale real estate construction and management with projects such as a modern housing development on land bounded
by Nanking, Chiukiang, and Szechuan Roads valued at 1,000,000
taels. The Ezra family hotels included the Astor House Hotel
which attracted a socially prominent clientele, although it was
later taken over by the Kadoorie interests. N. E. B. Ezra founded
and edited the Anglo-Jewish weekly newspaper, *Israel's Messenger*,
from 1909 to 1935, a publication which became the official
organ of the Shanghai Zionist movement.

Silas Hardoon alone among the Shanghai Jewry was not spo-
ken of as the head or a member of a family, but always as an
individual. There is so much information on him that it is
difficult to distinguish fact from fiction, but there is no doubt
that Hardoon was a colourful as well as interesting personality. He was also extremely wealthy. Although elected to the
Municipal Council of the International Settlement as well as
the Conseil municipal of the French Concession, it was under-
stood that Silas Hardoon purchased this honour by meeting
the cost of paving Nanking Road.

After World War II ended in 1945 the Jewish refugees from Europe left Shanghai to settle in the United States, Canada, Australia, or Israel; long-term residents left after the communist victory of 1949. Of the 543 Jews remaining in China in 1956, 231 of them were living in Shanghai. Out of the total, 402 were classified as Soviet citizens by the Chinese government and, in consequence, were not able to obtain the necessary papers to emigrate. R. D. Abraham, still leader of the Jewish community at that time, learned through a BBC broadcast that David Marshall, a noted Jewish lawyer from Singapore, was being invited to visit China. He wrote to Marshall, and asked him to intervene. The lawyer was able to speak to Premier Chou Enlai (Zhou Enlai) who initiated arrangements for the stranded group to leave China.

Only one Jewish woman, a 75-year old by the name of Agre, who although born in Russia was officially listed as stateless, remained in China by 1983. The last Jewish resident in Shanghai, a Max Lieberman, died in 1982.

6

Vestiges of Old Shanghai

SHANGHAI at the end of the twentieth century, noisy and over-crowded, remains vibrant still. The Bund, with buildings which have become architectural monuments to the city's more glorious days, has remained intact, and well-known streets, such as Nanking Road, also survive with few changes. As a result, the centre of the city at least continues to be recognizable to visitors who can remember Old Shanghai.

As the People's Liberation Army entered Shanghai in May 1949, many foreigners as well as Chinese residents left for Hong Kong or other places outside China. The number of British residents, for instance, dropped from 4,000 to 2,000 within a few weeks. From 14 May onwards, sounds of gunfire could be heard on the outskirts of the city. On 19 May, residents looking out of Broadway Mansions were flabbergasted by the sight below. Soochow Creek, ordinarily choked with traffic, was completely empty—'not one ship, not one junk, not one sampan'. On 24 May 1949, the Communist take-over of the city was complete, signalling the demise of Old Shanghai. Its former residents began to make contributions elsewhere. In Hong Kong alone, among other successes, they amassed the largest commercial shipping fleets in the world, and created the textile industry. They also supplied the territory with electric power, and produced garments, watches, and jewellery. The film industry, organized by the moguls of Old Shanghai, introduced *kung-fu* to the international vocabulary.

Metropolitan Shanghai has expanded considerably since 1949, with satellite towns spreading out in all directions. Housing has been constructed in these new towns to accommodate the population, officially estimated to be more than thirteen million in 1992 but, for reasons of convenience, many people have preferred to remain in the older areas. Consequently, what used to be single-family dwellings may today house one family in each room, and new buildings have been constructed where gardens and tennis courts formerly stood.

If the streets appear to need scrubbing and most buildings a fresh coat of paint, it is because Shanghai has had little funds for such surface beautification. Until 1985, the city—dominated by state industry—had to contribute between 85 and 86 per cent of its revenue to the central government in Peking. The remaining 14 to 15 per cent had to take care of salaries, administrative expenses and the upkeep of facilities and the infrastructure, as well as any development of outlying areas.

Shanghai's basic infrastructure of electricity, water, gas, and sewers, in place for more than a century and in desperate need of refurbishment and repair, are still in use. The Whangpoo is not deep enough to accommodate container ships; there is a serious problem of industrial pollution. In 1885, the Shanghai Water Company had supplied 412,199,739 gallons of 'eminently potable and high quality drinking water' to residents; by 1917, it was 5,208,612,897 gallons, and today, many of the original pipes are still in service. Electricity was adopted in the International Settlement in 1882, the French Concession in 1897, and Chinese Shanghai by 1898. Street lighting had begun in 1864 with lamps first lit with gas, then electricity. There is an obvious need for swift action to be taken to bring all these facilities up to modern standards.

The Old Shanghai Police Station, the scene of the May Thirtieth Incident of 1925 when policemen shot and

and killed demonstrating students and workers, still stands at a Nanking Road junction. A professional police force was first introduced to the International Settlement in 1854. The Volunteer Fire Brigade was organized in 1866 in the International Settlement and, shortly thereafter, in the French Concession. In 1889, paid firemen were added to the volunteers when the fire brigade came under the control of the Municipal Council and the Conseil municipal (Fig. 6.1).

OFFICERS IN THE SHANGHAI FIRE BRIGADE 1905.

1st Row	2nd Row	3rd Row
G. R. ANDERSON.	1. A. W. KIRSCHSTEIN	1. H. D. PARKHILL
W. F. SUHSMIHL.	(Foreman Mih-Ho-Loong Co.)	(Departmental Engin
C. J. SCOTT,	2. J. W. CAMERON	2. J. M. D. THOMAS.
(Foreman Victoria Co.)	Foreman Deluge Co.	3. P. VENUE.
J. C. BOSUSTOW.	3. G. S. V. BIDWELL	4. H. BAHLMANN.
H. WINBERG.	(Chief Engineer.)	
A. W. MACPHAIL.	4. A. W. COLOMB	
	(Foreman Le Torrent Co.)	
l from left to right.	5. W. NAGEL	
	(Foreman Hongkew Co.)	

Ir. Kahler joined the Shanghai Fire ade in 1871, and for many years was ng the most enthusiastic of its mem- —rising to the proud position of Chief

Mr. H. D. Parkhill, the Depart Engineer, has been a member Brigade since 1898, and is the owne long service medal. He was appoin his present position three years ago.

6.1
Officers of the Shanghai Fire Brigade in 1905.

6.2 The opening of the first railroad in China took place in Shanghai in 1867.

6.3 The rickshaw, introduced into Shanghai from Japan in 1874, became an instant success in the city.

The pre-1949 railway stations, renovated and expanded, still serve the travelling public. Railways supplemented ships for long-distance transportation of passengers and goods in China as occurred in countries throughout the world after the middle of the nineteenth century. The first railroad in China was built in Shanghai, linking Woosung and Kiangwan (Fig. 6.2). The line operated from 1867 to 1877 when a new line was constructed connecting the Yangtze Delta with the middle Yangtze cities. Early modes of local transportation had ranged from sedan chairs carried by coolies to single-wheeled carts which apparently were relatively safe and comfortable. The rickshaw, the invention that symbolized the mysterious Orient in many Western minds, was introduced from Japan in 1874 (Fig. 6.3). Horse-drawn carriages came from the West and were immediately popular among a wide cross-section of the Shanghai Chinese. In 1895, two automobiles were imported, and by 1912 the major roads in Shanghai were already paved. Tram and trolley brought public transport to the foreign settlements in 1908. Ten years later there were ninety tramcars, seventy trailers, and seven cars without rails, traversing a track of 16.4 miles. The Garden Bridge across Soochow Creek was built in 1909 to accommodate automobiles, its predecessor, the Willis Bridge, in place since the early days of the International Settlement, being deemed too steep for this mode of transport. In June 1889, a three-day survey was taken of the amount of traffic which crossed Willis Bridge:

Type of Vehicle

Single-wheeled carts	2,759
Carriages	1,633
Rickshaws	20,958
Lorries (goods vehicles)	22
Sedan chairs	27
Horses	38

Apart from a wide variety of buildings, other vestiges of Old Shanghai remain. To rid the city of its imperialist past and to reflect the character of new China, the names of many streets have been changed. Those named for a Chinese province or city, however, have retained their old labels. The Bund, an Indian term for embankment or quay adopted by the British in the Far East, remains as such in English, as does its Chinese name, Wai-t'an (Waitan)—the Foreshore. Other streets with foreign associations have been re-named. Rue de Consulat in the French Concession is now Jinling Road East. Bubbling Well Road of the International Settlement, named after a well situated outside the main gate of a Buddhist temple that foreigners had dubbed the Bubbling Well Temple, is now called Nanjing Road West.

Some of the hotels of Old Shanghai that gained world renown still operate as such. The Cathay Hotel (Sassoon House) facing the Bund, is today known as the Peace Hotel. Its ballroom, venue of many elegant dances in past eras, is now a restaurant serving Western food. The Park Hotel, built in 1934, has regained its old name, however, after a period as the International Hotel. Broadway Mansions, apartments that housed American officers in the days immediately after the end of World War II, is now a hotel named Shanghai Mansions.

The centrally located Shanghai race-course was turned into the People's Park. The Ohel Moshe Synagogue in Hongkew is now the isolation ward of the Shanghai Mental Hospital. A photograph taken in 1984 of the Beth Aharon Synagogue shows the dome of the house of worship intact but the Star of David covered by a coat of paint. The United States government was asked to intercede to have the whole synagogue preserved but, even so, the building no longer exists. The Jewish cemetery was demolished during the

Cultural Revolution although its chapel still stood as late as 1983, but used as a tea house. Hardoon's Aili Garden became the Shanghai Agricultural Exhibition Hall, while the Marble Hall that belonged to the Kadoorie family is a large Children's Palace used for after-school activities.

Some buildings housing educational, religious and cultural institutions have been turned to other uses; others have remained intact. A large number of major colleges and universities still operate under their pre-1949 names, such as Fudan University. Other missionary foundations have had their names changed, but otherwise still function as educational institutions. The popular Buddhist shrines that have survived include the Bubbling Well Temple and the Jade Buddha Temple. The Temple of the City God, for decades an arts and crafts store, has now been converted back to its original purpose. The Roman Catholic cathedral in Siccawei was re-opened in 1979 as a house of worship, followed by a number of Protestant churches and the Mosque. All the public parks continue to exist as recreation grounds. The former Wing-On and Sincere department store buildings are still in operation as shops, but with different names.

The Shanghai Museum of Art on Museum Road and the Museum of Natural History in Siccawei remain fine institutions today. The collection of books, supplemented by newer volumes, from the Shanghai Library survives. On the other hand, the tradition of publishing has been moderated. Although the leading publishers, such as the Commercial Press, the People's Publications, and Zhonghua Book Company, have remained active, the dozens of newspapers published in pre-1949 Shanghai in Chinese, Japanese, and Western languages have been long discontinued.

The French Club, now the Jingjiang Club, did not have

chilled champagne on hand in 1984 to serve to Joan Carroll Baker on her return; someone who had been presented to society in its ballroom in the late 1930s. The night clubs of Old Shanghai, many of which, in the words of a contemporary writer, were places of 'joy, gin, and jazz' featuring Chinese, Japanese, Korean, Eurasian, Russian, and other 'dancing hostesses and gigolos' at a dime to a dollar a dance; are no longer in evidence. They have been replaced by modern, but often seedy, establishments featuring karaoke and rock 'n roll.

One of the most nostalgic old buildings on the Bund for Europeans who remember Old Shanghai, the Shanghai Club, is the Dongfeng (East Wind) Hotel, which is used primarily by visiting cadres and their families. The 110-foot bar, originally the longest in the world, is now divided into three sections at which ice cream and fizzy drinks are served. The Russian Consulate, located on Soochow Creek facing Garden Bridge, until recently used as municipal offices, has been returned to its former owners. The Hongkong and Shanghai Bank building, however, remains the headquarters of the People's Government of the Municipality of Shanghai. The American Consulate is again occupied by the United States Consulate, but buildings in the British Consulate complex have not been re-alloted to Great Britain.

Today, Shanghai is lagging behind other areas of China in attracting new investment. The Pearl River Delta just north of Hong Kong, and even towns along the lower Yangtze in Kiangsu province, are surging ahead. While the Pearl River Delta is being promoted as Asia's Fifth Little Dragon—linking it to the four spectacular economies of Hong Kong, Singapore, South Korea, and Taiwan—Shanghai's growth rate is falling behind that of Kiangsu. In 1991, the coastal province of Kwangtung attracted 45 per cent of China's foreign investment capital commitments, while Shanghai received four per cent, about US$400 million.

As might be expected from a city with a history of commercial success, steps have been taken to increase capital commitment and investment facilities in Shanghai. An interbank short-term credit market and a securities exchange were opened in 1986. Five years later it was estimated that more than one million people played the stock market. Programmes have been implemented to develop Pootung as an industrial era, concentrating on heavy industries and light manufacturing. Foreign investment is being actively encouraged, with the Singer Company, for instance, acquiring in 1992 a 70 per cent stake in the leading local sewing machine manufacturer to produce industrial sewing machines. Since the beginning of the twentieth century 'Singer sewing machine' has been a household word in Shanghai, and a coveted item for every woman's hope-chest. A retail shop for domestic sewing machines is planned for Nanking Road.

There are also plans to deepen the harbour to accommodate container shipping, as well as for a bridge to link Pootung with the docks and railroad terminals of Shanghai. Nevertheless, Shanghai still has a long way to go before it can even hope to regain the status it enjoyed before 1949 as the country's leading financial, commercial, and industrial centre.

Selected Bibliography

SOURCES IN ENGLISH

All About Shanghai and Environs: A Standard Guidebook (Shanghai, The University Press, 1934–5.)

Cambridge History of China, Vol. 11, Denis Twitchett and J. K. Fairbank (eds.); Vol. 13, J. K. Fairbank and Albert Feuerwerker (eds.), (Cambridge: Cambridge University Press, 1980–6).

Darwent, C. E., *Shanghai: A Handbook for Travellers and Residents*, second edition (Shanghai, Kelly and Walsh, 1920).

Economist, The, April 11–17, 1992, pp. 26–7.

Elvin, Mark, 'Market Towns and Waterways: The County of Shang-hai from 1480 to 1910', in G. William Skinner (eds.), *Chinese City Between Two Worlds* (Stanford, Stanford University Press, 1974).

Feuerwerker, Albert, *The Foreign Establishment in China in the Early Twentieth Century*, Michigan Papers in Chinese Studies No. 29 (Ann Arbor, 1976).

Johnson, Linda Cooke, 'Shanghai: an Emerging Jiangnan Port 1683–1840', in Linda Cooke Johnson (eds.), *Cities of Jiangnan: Studies in the Urban History of Late Imperial China*, (Albany, State University of New York Press, 1992).

Shanghai of To-day, a Souvenir Album of Fifty Vandyck Prints of 'the Model Settlement'., with an introduction by O.M. Green, editor of the *North China Daily News*, second edition, (Shanghai: Kelly and Walsh, 1928).

Wei, Betty Peh-T'i, *Shanghai: Crucible of Modern China* (Hong Kong, Oxford University Press, 1987)

SOURCES IN CHINESE

Guo Chuyin 郭緒印 et. al., *Jiu Shanghai he sheguimishi* 舊上海黑社會秘史 [*Secret societies of old Shanghai*],(Anyang: Henan People's Publishing, 1991).

Liu Huiwu 劉惠吾 et. al., *Shanghai jindai shi* 上海近代史 [*History of modern Shanghai*] (Shanghai: Huadong Teachers' University Publishing, 1985–7).

Shanghai 700 nian 上海七百年 [*Seven hundred years of Shanghai*], compiled by the Centre for Shanghai Studies (Shanghai: People's Publishing, 1991).

Shanghai zhinan 上海指南 [*Guide to Shanghai*], compiled by the Editorial and Translation Department of the Commercial Press (Shanghai, Commercial Press, 1920).

Shanghai yanjiu ziliao 上海研究資料 [*Collection of materials for historical research on Shanghai*] (Shanghai: Shanghai Tongshe, 1935).

Tang Zhenchang 唐振常 (ed) et. al., *Shanghai shi* 上海史 [*History of Shanghai*], compiled by the Institute of History, Academy of Social Science of Shanghai (Shanghai, People's Publishing, 1989).

Wu Guifang 吳貴芳(ed) et.al., *Shanghai fengwuzhi* 上海風物志 [*Customs and traditions of Shanghai*] (Shanghai: Wenhua Publishing, 1985).

Xu Min, 許敏 'Shi, Chang, You-wan Qing Shanghai shehui shenghe yibi' 士娼優—晚清社會生活一瞥 [Scholars, Courtesans and Actors - A glimpse into an aspect of social life in Shanghai during the late Qing era], paper presented at the International Symposium on Urban Studies to mark the 700th anniversary of the founding of Shanghai (Shanghai, October 1991).

Index/Glossary

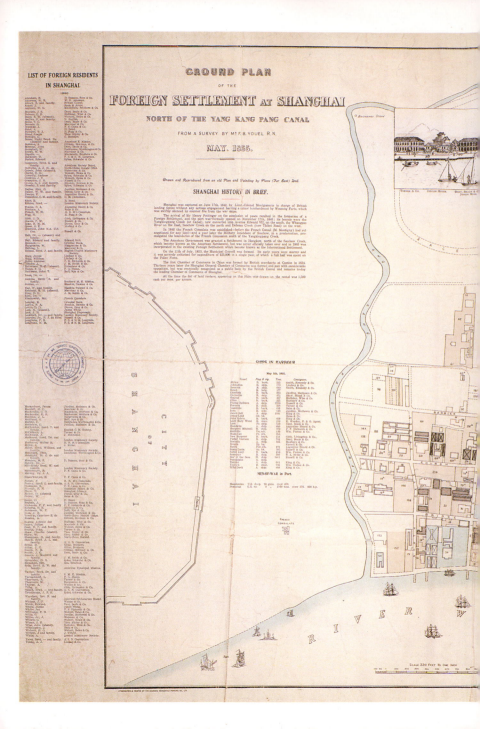